The Universe is my Sugar Daddy

Ryin Amber Lokietz

ISBN: 9780578833804

I want to give an enormous thank you to all the beautiful souls that have helped me to create this piece of art in the physical (Moxy, Angela, Sean), and all of my friends and family that have been here for me to hype me up during this entire process!
THANK YOU!!

I also want to thank all of the people, places and things (including the pandemic and other fucked up shit of the past) that have inspired me along my journey and have gotten me to where I am today.

Sending some extra gratitude for my guides, my angels and my biggest supporter: my sugar daddy, The Universe.

CONTENTS

FOREWORD

Wouldn't it be nice if you didn't have to worry about money? If someone paid all your bills and took you to fancy dinners? Bought you presents and gifts, made you feel like the most beautiful and well-taken-care-of girl in the world... and all you had to do is *be yourself*???? Well, I'm not actually suggesting you go out seeking a Sugar Daddy—although I don't judge if you're into that kind of thing—I'm saying you already have one! The biggest, wealthiest, most supportive, loving, caring kind of Sugar Daddy any gal could ever ask for. He pays your bills before they're due, makes you feel loved, secure and safe, and is always there when you need him. His name is the Universe. And YES girl, he is here for you.

In this book, we are going to go through all the reasons why, maybe, you think your "Sugar Daddy," aka the Universe, is not taking care of you, and we're going to get you some well deserved allowance!!!

SUGAR DADDY??

So what is a *Sugar Daddy*?

A more gender neutral term coined by millennials is *glucose guardian*. But for the sake of this book, I'm just going to use the term *Sugar Daddy*, so get comfortable.

According to Dictionary.com a *Sugar Daddy* is "a wealthy, middle-aged man who spends freely on a young woman in return for her companionship or intimacy."

Urbandictionary says a *Sugar Daddy* is "Like a genie- he may be a little old, but if a girl rubs his lamp, he'll grant her wishes."

LOL

This topic is definitely a polarizing one.

And it probably makes you cringe while getting you a little curious at the same time.

There were thousands of questions rolling through my mind when I first heard about the concept... all the typical questions a young and financially struggling adult might ask while they're on the verge of their 9th mental breakdown of the morning...

I know I'm not the only girl who has had at least the tiniest urge to escape life and bills to jump into the arms of an older gentleman; hence the reason why I wrote this book.

I never had rich parents. They never even helped me with a single bill in my life! At the beginning of my journey, I used to hate the lucky fuckin' kids whose parents bought them their first car and paid for their college. I used to think the Universe totally fucked me over by burdening me with guardians who weren't able to provide me the material things that a lot of other kids' parents were providing for them.

Let's just say that I was living in Struggle City for a long ass time, in fact, I was basically the mayor!

Ever since I was 20, I've had this idea whispering to me from the back of my mind. When times got tough, I'd hear a little voice calling out to me, "Ryin, if only you had a Sugar Daddy, life would be so much easier!" And times did get tough. I was even homeless at one point, believe it or not. I wasn't sleeping on a park bench or anything, but I was hopping from couch to couch to garage to my car. It's been a wild journey! I'm not trying to justify where I've been or make you pity me, I'm simply offering my story as living proof that, even in desperate times, there's always a way out. Throughout my journey I have come to realize that everything really does happen for a reason.

It's up to YOU and ME to find out what that reason is.

Our perspective is the most important thing we can learn to control in this life. When you master that, you will see that the whole entire Universe is actually on your side.

I wouldn't change a single thing in my life, especially knowing now that it's brought me to where I am today, writing this book for you.

WARNING: I am not going to teach you how to be a good sugar baby.

What I am here to share with you is **the secret of the Universe**, and why you will never have to fuck an old guy for money, ever. (Unless that's your kink or something, but that's a totally different story that I'm not going to get into today… no judgement here girlfriend!!)

There is a place within each of us where the entire Universe dwells. A place of peace, love and joy. When you are in that place within you and when I am in that place within me, we are one.

The word Universe, which I will be using a lot in this book, is the term I use to describe the vast network of energy that connects all humans and things. This energy creates worlds, and can also be referred to as Source, God, or any number of names. When I began my spiritual journey, I really liked to use 'Universe' because I felt like it captured the wholeness of it all. It really doesn't matter which term you prefer, but it IS important to remember this: we are ALL connected by this infinitely abundant energy source. The energy that brings life to my body is the same energy that brings life to yours. When I am connected to this energy source, things are in flow. This flow state is a magical place to be because, in this state, the entire Universe is conspiring to make everything work out for me. And when you're in the flow, the whole Universe is conspiring to make everything work out for you, too. Like catching every green light or scoring the best parking spaces everywhere you go.

This is the *Sugar Daddy energy* I'm talking about here. From this flow state, everything is possible. Whatever can go right, will go right. Throughout this book, I'm going to be bouncing back and forth between spiritual lingo and Sugar Daddy talk, but I want you to understand the relevance.

THE UNIVERSE IS ALWAYS HERE FOR US AS LONG AS WE'RE LISTENING.

The problem is that we typically are not taught to connect with or listen to the Universe. Our society conditions us to think and act in certain ways, like thinking we have to work hard and that happiness comes at a cost, which isn't true at all. We actually have the power to do whatever we fucking want with our lives. Wanna be a millionaire? Why not?! Wouldn't it be awesome if you woke up tomorrow and looked in the mirror, only to see the millionaire best version of yourself staring back at you? What would be different in your life? This IS fucking possible but a lot of us give up before we even give ourselves a chance to get there! What would you be willing to do in order to make this big dream a reality? Would you be willing to replace your old beliefs with new ones?

The thing is, our minds only have so much room. Do you hear thousands of thoughts going on inside your head at any given moment? I know I do, and it's hella distracting! Well, these thoughts and beliefs are all based on everything we've been told and everything we've experienced since birth, and some of them are outdated AF!

It's up to us to release the thoughts and beliefs that are no longer serving us in order to create more space for what we truly desire.

Imagine this: your Sugar Daddy buys you your dream car! You manifested it, and now it is here! You drive it off the lot and pull up to your house only to see your old busted car you've been driving since high school still parked in the driveway. There's no street parking in your entire neighborhood, and there's only enough room for one car in the driveway.

What do you do? You finally have the car of your dreams but nowhere to park it.

What are you gonna do?

You've gotta get rid of the old car, right?

Well that's easier said than done. You have lots of memories in that old car. You two have been through so much together over the years. It's probably hard to say goodbye.

Some of you might say, "Heck yeah! Get rid of the old car! My new and beautiful dream car is finally here!"

And that's the kind of attitude I want to see when we start releasing these old beliefs. It's not that these old beliefs are even all bad, it's just that they've had their time to serve you, and now they're holding you behind from your greatness.

Your beliefs about the Universe may need some upgrading as well; especially if you believe life is hard or that you can't do this all on your own.

But you don't have to worry! You aren't doing this alone anymore. I am here with you. And even better than me, our Sugar Daddy, the Universe, is here too. ;)

SUGAR DATING

So imagine this:

Your Sugar Daddy takes you out to a fancy dinner. He drives you there in your dream sports car. A real gentleman, he holds the restaurant door open for you as you walk in looking as glamorous as ever, wearing the most stunning outfit (which he bought you btw), feeling very boujee and beautiful. During dinner, he invites you to order whatever you'd like, he's buying, and you feast on the most delicious mouth watering plate of your favorite meal.

"How's your food?" Sugar Daddy asks sincerely. You don't answer him. You're busy texting your friends about how much of a loser he is (even though you didn't even give him a chance to impress you in the first place). You avoid his attempts to engage with you and treat him like he doesn't exist. When the bill comes, you don't even bat an eye or thank him, but he covers it anyway, eager to treat you well, ever the gentleman. You tell him that you're going to the restroom, but really you call an uber and leave out the back door. He waits at the table, excited for your return, and then the minutes turn into hours. He wants to know that you're okay, but mostly, he doesn't want to eat dessert alone.

How do you think your Sugar Daddy feels? Neglected? Sad? Disappointed? Upset? Lonely? He probably doesn't want to take you out ever again...

But then, lo and behold, here you are just a few days later, texting him, "omg my car needs new tires will you please help me out? *insert kissy face and crying face emojis*"

Do you think that if you were him, you'd immediately start venmoing over tire money? Probably not, right?

Girl I want you to know that the Universe is here and taking special care of you every step of the way, but if you neglect and deprive him like you just did that imaginary Sugar Daddy, then it's no wonder you ain't gettin' a break (aka rollin' around in the monayyy) yet.

Let's take a step back and look at the relationship you have with the Universe (and money) right here, right now, and look at some things that could be holding you back from your unlimited divine wealth. Ask yourself:

1. Are you showing gratitude for everything the Universe is doing for you?
2. Are you noticing all the millions of tiny gestures (aka mini miracles) that are going on in your life?
3. Do you neglect the Universe by not spending time together (or alone: to meditate, journal or pray)?
4. Do you speak poorly of the Universe (and money) to the point where abundance doesn't want to be your friend?
5. Are you holding onto past relationships (aka old disagreements and drama), bringing those heavy emotions into your new relationships (aka not clearing your heart chakra and allowing it to be filled with love, light and abundance), and bringing unnecessary strain and stress into your life?

If you answered yes to any of these tough questions, I don't want you to freak out. These are all things that we can release and learn to do better. I'm proud of you for reading this far and for having the interest in taking an energetic step on the journey to unlimited divine abundance.

COUPLES THERAPY

The first thing we have to remember here is that this relationship goes both ways. Sugar Daddy provides but YOU gotta AT LEAST say thank you!

The practice of Gratitude has changed my life. I started a Gratitude journal a few years ago, triggering the biggest positive shift for me on my journey, which is why I am sharing the concept with you now.

I don't want you to think you need to switch your whole life up in order for the Universe to be here supporting you and giving you all the sugar you desire, but I do want this book to inspire you to want to connect to the Universe more deeply so that you can experience the joy and love that I have.

Mending my relationship with the Universe has changed my life entirely, and for me, it all started with Gratitude.

When you are grateful, fear disappears and abundance appears.

GRATITUDE is a very transformative energy. A little 'thanks' goes a long way.

Imagine your sugar date from the last chapter. Let's say before the date, you're at the mall shopping for an outfit. You're excited for dinner and you get a text from Sugar Daddy saying he's looking forward to tonight. You tell him how excited you are to see him and that you're out shopping in preparation. He sends you the money for the gorgeous outfit you're about to buy. He can't wait to see it.

Time for dinner, and he picks you up in your favorite dream car. He holds the door open for you, always the gentleman. You thank him and compliment his car and new haircut. During the ride to the restaurant, he plays one of his favorite songs, telling you it's been his favorite for over 20 years and will never get old! You agree, it's a classic.

You arrive at dinner, and of course, he holds the door open for you. You thank him, and he leads you to a nice fancy table with an amazing view of the city. He tells you to pick whatever you'd like off of the menu, and you thank him for taking you to your favorite restaurant. When you're halfway through your meal, he asks if you're enjoying it, which of course you are, so you tell him how delicious it is and ask if he's enjoying his meal. The conversation flows easily as you take turns sharing stories, telling jokes, and asking each other questions. After dinner, you excuse yourself to the restroom, and on the way back, you tip the live band to request Sugar Daddy's favorite song.

You come back to the table and dessert has arrived, just as the live band starts playing his favorite tune.

Look at the smile on Sugar Daddy's face! How do you think he's feeling?

I'll tell you what, I bet he's really enjoying himself. I'm sure if you needed to ask for anything right now he'd send it over without hesitation. He's so happy that you've taken the time to give him some attention and actually cared to listen to him talk, remembered his favorite song, and kept up with conversation during the whole date.

We all want to feel appreciated. And on this date, you made sure to show Sugar Daddy that you truly appreciated him.

At this point, anything you could ask for, he would give to you without hesitation. You've done an excellent job of showing him that you care and that you're thankful that he took you out.

So the point of this story is to show you that your Sugar Daddy has been doing a lot for you this whole time, and would be willing to do even more for you if you would just put a little effort into showing him the appreciation and love he deserves.

This is the same with the Universe. Okay, the Universe woke you up this morning. You've got a warm bed and a roof over your head. Even if you're homeless at the moment, you've still got air filling your lungs, or something to be grateful for. In Dale Carnegie's book, *How to Stop Worrying and Start Living*, he tells a story about a woman who was completely blind in her right eye and has only 20% visibility through one hole in her left eye. When she read, she had to hold the book so close to her face that her eyelashes touch the page. She didn't let her limited vision stop her though, and she went through school without letting people treat her like she was disabled. She studied all day and night, looking through that tiny peep hole, holding books up to her face to read them and actually graduated college with very high prestige. Some time later, when she was in her 40's, new technology made it possible for her to have an operation that allowed her to see 40% more out of her left eye! She can finally see things like the little rainbows in soap bubbles, so doing the dishes brings her joy now! Even though she only has 60% vision in ONE eye now, she spent so much of her life nearly blind that now she smiles so big with gratitude when she washes the dishes. Most people freaking hate the dishes!

Can you see how her perspective has gotten her so far?

There are millions of things to be grateful for all around us. And we can train our minds to look and find them.

If you want the Universe to keep taking care of you, start by saying thank you.

Here are some ways that I like to practice gratitude in my daily life, and YES, GRATITUDE SHOULD HAPPEN DAILY!!!!!!! Every minute of every day if you can! The more grateful you are, the more joy you'll experience, and the more amazing things will start happening to you.

Find out which gratitude practice you like best and start focusing time and energy on it every single day. Below are a few suggestions. Try one each day or switch it up. There is no right or wrong way to be grateful. Feel free to do whichever feels most natural to you. You can even create your own gratitude rituals. Make sure you are being intentional about it, not just choosing the easiest way to get it over with. This practice is going to change your life. So be happy, be grateful, and have fun!

Gratitude rituals to try:

- Every morning and night write down 10 things you're grateful for
- Every morning and night write down just a few things you're thankful for and why these things are so meaningful to you
- Start a gratitude journal and free write a page or more every day
- All day long, in your head or out loud, thank the Universe for all of your many blessings
- Tell the people in your life that you're thankful for them
- Challenge yourself to find something to be grateful for in situations that are testing you
- Write a love letter to the Universe thanking it for all of your many blessings

I've read some books that have given me "homework" that I wish I would have done. I like to listen to audio books, so sometimes I'm on the road or in the middle of things and don't have the chance to slow down and take the exercises seriously.

It's one thing to hear or read about it and another thing to actually BE about it.

If you're not going to stop what you're doing right now to find some time to be grateful, I'd like you to set a reminder in your phone to do it later instead. I know that we're all busy, but if you don't make the time, you will never find the time.

QUALITY TIME

Remember your date with Sugar Daddy? The one where you took the time to show him that you care? That scenario ended much more happily than the first one, right?

When we want to show the Universe that we care, we need to spend some QUALITY TIME with the Universe.

And quite frankly that means time alone.

Now, we can participate in group meditations and full moon gatherings with our witchy friends too, but particularly I mean it's time to start listening to our own internal guidance (aka our higher self).

When you spend time alone in quiet contemplation, you begin to tap into the unlimited answers from the Universe.

Some of us may not "hear" anything at first and that's okay. It's more about just incorporating quiet time to meditate and practice other spiritual routines everyday.

It doesn't have to be 30 whole minutes every single day, unless you want it to be. The more time you spend every day, the faster you'll be able to "hear" from your higher self. The reason why I keep putting the word "hear" in quotes is because technically this place of inner awareness is the space within us that is beyond all of the senses. We cannot hear, touch, taste, see, or smell this "one-ness" but we will eventually learn that it is there.

It's that quiet inner space within us that everything IS. It's within that space that we are whole, and where everything we desire is already done. It's from this space that the Universe speaks to us and, if we can practice listening, we will be able to hear what we want to know.

For those of you who don't really think meditation and alone time is important, I want you to think about this: in one single day in 2009, studies show that each of us intake 34 gigabytes of information! From 1980 to 2008, the number of bytes we consumed had increased 6 percent each year. Over 28 years, that's a 350 percent increase according to Andrew Nusca from ZDNet in 2009. Imagine how much more we are taking in now, nearly 10 years later! Our minds are always racing from one thing to the next. The time we have in between stressful situations is filled with social media and tv, so our brains never have a moment to rest.

A lot of us like to live this way because quieting the mind would mean facing the truth.

The truth is that most people are not happy. They are not happy because they are not living their lives in alignment with their soul's purpose.

A lot of us don't know what our soul's purpose is yet, but we don't have to know right away. As long as we make an effort to tune in to our higher selves, we WILL find our purpose along the way.

Think about the most badass version of yourself in another reality. What is she wearing? What is she doing? Is she living her life on a yacht sipping margaritas while her passive income streams bring in mega money? Is she a singer, traveling from venue to venue, sharing her love and talent with the world? Is she helping feed and clothe children in third world countries?

What is her soul crying to do?

There is probably something that your soul is crying to do right now, too.

I want you to think of every great story you've ever heard. Now, a lot of great stories are about a *hero* who travels far and wide to save the city from impending doom, almost dies a few times, wins a battle (or a few), and finally comes back alive to save whatever they went off to save in the first place.

A hero has enough strength for two and always chooses the battle that's as big as his or her soul.

Imagine if the hero didn't fight the dragon. Imagine if the hero decided that it would be cool to just stay home and let the city crumble.

The movie, *The Revenant*, follows its hero's extreme journey through Alaska to get revenge on a man who murdered his son. In this film, the main character (Leonardo DiCaprio) endures many near death experiences, including being attacked by a bear, falling off of a cliff while on horseback, literally almost freezing to death and lots more. Now, I'm not saying this is my favorite movie or anything, but imagine if he would have just died in the beginning of the movie? There would be no movie at all!

Sometimes in life, we're hit with one big challenge and then the next and then the next. In fact, our whole dang lives are really just a combination of the stories we tell.

WE ARE THE HEROES OF OUR OWN LIVES.

How we tell the story is up to us.

When I was 18 I got arrested, and I blamed it on everything and everyone else around me. I said that these people screwed me over, so that's why I was in the situation that I was in. To be honest, I wasn't really hanging out with the "right crowd" and it took me a while to shift the way I saw my situation and told my story.

Back then, my story went like this: My BF at the time and I had just gotten a new apartment, we both had great jobs (lol not really but back then we really thought we did) and I was finishing up high school. Everything seemed great. Until late one night, our friend's twin brother got robbed at gunpoint at their house. For some reason, probably because they were on a drug binge at the time, they blamed my BF and our neighbor for the robbery and retaliated by breaking into our neighbors' apartment. They got arrested and, while in custody, they claimed my BF had been the one who robbed them at gunpoint first, so the cops came to my house to investigate. I was at work at the time, but my BF and his buddy were smoking a fat joint, which gave the officers "probable cause" to enter my home and arrest my BF, accusing him of attempted murder for the gunpoint robbery he didn't commit. He was 17 at the time, and as a minor he could not come out on bail.

When I got home from work that day, my friends were really upset about everything that happened and, blaming our mutual friend for my BF's arrest, decided to go jump him in the parking lot at his work. I didn't know that's where they were going at the time, but I went with them because I didn't want to stay home alone. Later on, I was arrested for what happened that night in the parking lot with 'principle to battery' and 'tampering with/harassing a witness'. Everyone had the whole story completely wrong. The police report said that I fled the city, and nobody knew what the fuck they were talking about. The dates didn't even match up for anything at all. We had to hire a lawyer for my BF so he could come home. I hired a lawyer for my own reasons. It turned out that the two different cases that had been mistakenly linked, but at the end of the day, I was just fucking pissed that I had been doing so great until everyone else got messy and fucked my life up for no damn reason.

I lived in that energy for many years. I hated those people for screwing up everything. I felt like if it hadn't been for them, we wouldn't have spent so much time paying off legal fees. We lived on my BF's brother's couch for a while because we'd been kicked out of our apartment. I was bullied in school by members of the other crew, and because all of my friends were actually drop outs, I didn't have anyone at school to help defend me. I lost my job at the preschool because you can't work with children when you have a felony on your record. That job was tied to my grade in one of my classes, so losing the job meant I failed the class. I graduated high school but that one failed class means I lost my 'bright futures' college scholarship. I felt like my whole life plan was fucked, all because of these idiot drug dealing kids.

I tell that story a little differently now: I know that I was put in that situation to learn a lesson. Luckily, I was safe, and, thanks to my amazing lawyer, the charges were dropped, leaving my record completely clean. I was able to help my BF pay off his aunt who was gracious enough to pay his lawyer for him when we didn't have the money. I got my job back at the preschool and got hired as a server at a local bar during my time between jobs. I worked at that bar for about five years, and became part of the Ruby Street Grille family. I ended friendships with the toxic people in my life and learned to forgive them.

I have no hate for anyone that was involved anymore. I have learned that we ARE who we hang out with, and back then, I was just hanging out with a bunch of pot smoking teenagers with no motivation or real ambition to go anywhere in life, so now I really prioritize making friendships with people who have similar values to me. I think a lot of my old friends eventually cleaned up and got their shit together, one of them being my ex BF.

I'm also thankful to my BF's mom, Angel, who literally is an angel, for helping me get through those tough times. My ex and I grew apart and separated a few years later, but I have no hard feelings toward him and am so grateful that he did not get charged for attempted murder either. That part of my life was hard. It was so hard, but it taught me to be strong, street smart, humble, grateful, forgiving, and persistent. And it also showed me that back then, I was not living in alignment with my higher self or my soul purpose. I smoked a lot of Mary Jane, and I now see that I was using it to numb the fact that I wasn't living my purpose. Now, I have more **awareness of my intention**, especially if I smoke weed or partake in any other type of mind altering substances. Awareness and intention are really really important, and I may not have learned that if I had stayed on the path I was on when I was younger. Still, without that chaotic chain of events, I would not be where I am today.

Look at that. I changed the whole story just by changing my **perspective**. I'm grateful for my past and how it's shaped me into who I am today.

How we tell our story matters. In the first version of my story, I was the **victim**. And in the second version of the story, I was the **hero**.

How are you telling YOUR story? Are you playing hero or are you playing victim? It's okay to be both, but just know that it is OUR OWN RESPONSIBILITY to stand the fuck up and start being our own hero eventually.

Fuck eventually! Let's start writing the new story now!!

Say it with me, "I AM WRITING A NEW STORY FOR MYSELF AND I AM THE MOTHAFUCKIN HERO!"

Let that sink in! You don't have to play victim anymore!!!!! Every single thing we desire IS within our reach. If I want to be a superstar, I can! If I want to be a millionaire, I fucking can! And the same goes for you!

Our souls are an extension of the Universe. And the Universe is infinitely abundant. So that means that our souls want more than just a mediocre life.

Most people are comfortable where they are. They aren't willing to change because change will take them outside of their comfort zone. But it is right outside of the comfort zone that growth actually happens.

Most people are afraid to change, grow and heal because their entire identity is centered around the trauma they've experienced. They don't know who they are outside of their trauma and they're scared of the unknown.

We are all scared of the unknown. But the people who want to grow and live to the fullest expression of their souls know that stepping outside of their comfort zone is how they will get closer and closer to where they want to be.

Remember that we can all be heroes, or we can all be victims, depending on our perspective and how we tell the story.

Our life is a series of stories and we are the authors. Is your story, "this happened and it took me down, and now I can't get up…" or is the story you tell, "this happened and I fell down, but I got up, and I didn't let it stop me!"

The second story is about a true hero, and we all have the power within us to change our lives. When we sit in the quiet of our minds, we learn to tap into this energy and power and tune in to our higher selves. Our highest self can do no wrong because it is always moving from a place of unconditional love. From this place we have no fear, and we will always be willing to move outside of our comfort zones to rise to the epic battle that our inner hero came to fight.

Our higher self is our hero. And we find this hero when we take time to listen to its guidance.

Fear = absence of love

When I am scared, I understand that it means that I need to connect to my higher self and the Universe more deeply. When I am standing strong in my vibration of love, nothing can scare me. And whenever something does scare me, I know that I have the strength and power to overcome it by trusting in the Universe.

"Listen to the silence. It has so much to say."
~Rumi

Meditation is more about the practice of *listening* than anything else. When you try to tune into this silent place, you'll probably notice that it's usually not silent at all. This is where most people get frustrated and say that meditation isn't for them.

It's this moment of quieting the mind that is the most uncomfortable for a lot of us. The thoughts that consume us all day long are finally sitting alone with no music or noise to cover them up.

How can I listen for divine guidance with all this chatter going on inside here?

I know that for the first few YEARS of my spiritual practice I barely even meditated, although I wish I had. I wanted to meditate, I knew that I "should" have been meditating, but I was scared. Or uncomfortable. I don't know what it was, but the chatter in my mind did not want to shut up (EVER!) so I always felt like I was doing it wrong. I felt discouraged, which made me lack confidence in myself, which took me further away from my purpose.

Then, I got lucky and started dating a guy who meditates everyday. I started meditating with him, and from then on, my practice has grown. I *finally* LOVE this simple but OH SO POWERFUL tool that once caused me so much frustration.

Meditation may seem overwhelming at first, but with practice, it will become much easier.

Meditation is simple. Don't make it hard.

The hardest part is making the commitment to sit down and do it. Then, it's just about breathing and trying to relax.

Just sit in a quiet place where you will not be distracted. Put your phone away. Get comfortable.

You can sit up with a tall spine or lie down flat on your back, whichever is more comfortable for you. They say sitting up tall helps the energy to flow as if your body is a channel for divine energy. I prefer to sit because I usually fall asleep when I lie down.

When we go into a meditative state, our brain produces Alpha waves. When we are awake our brain waves are Beta, and when we sleep they go into either Delta or Theta, depending on how deep we go. Some say it doesn't matter which waves you're producing while meditating, but I find the best results from meditating when I'm awake and producing Alpha waves.

That said, there is no wrong way to practice meditation. Remember that it's a practice, so however you're doing it, you're doing it right!!!

So sit up or lie down, get comfortable and relaxed.

You can set a timer on your phone or use a meditation app (*Insight Timer* is a WONDERFUL free app, or you can try *Headspace* which is great for beginners).

If this is your first time meditating, just set the timer to 5 minutes and close your eyes.

Know that you are safe and protected by love and light.

If you feel scared, you can imagine white light surrounding you for protection while your eyes are closed.

Now take a moment to relax again and start taking deep breaths.

Just get really calm and relaxed.

There are going to be thoughts that come up in your mind, and that's okay.

When each thought comes into your mind, you can notice that it is there, and then just relax and let it go.

If you find space between the thoughts try to focus on that space. It will grow longer and longer over time, but try not to get attached to "if you're doing it right".

Keep it up until the timer goes off. After a couple sessions, maybe you turn the timer up to 10 or 15 minutes. Practicing meditation every day, even for just 5 minutes, is going to change your life. As long as you're PRACTICING meditation, you ARE doing it right.

It's easiest for me to meditate first thing in the morning before anything else distracts me and I forget.

Do you have 5 minutes to spare TODAY?

Do you think you can take 5 minutes out of your day to connect with the Universe every day?

How much time can you commit?

If you're saying, "no, 5 minutes is too much time. I'm far too busy for 5 minutes," then maybe we need to reevaluate where your priorities are. Open the settings on your phone and look at your total screen time. If you're spending over 4 hours on your phone every day like me, you may notice that "not having enough time" isn't the problem.

Sometimes we blame things like "not having time" when the truth is we are scared to go within.

It's okay to be scared and you're totally not alone. In fact, there are probably hundreds of thousands of people out there who are scared to go within to find the answers they seek.

It is okay to be scared. It's not okay to let fear stand in your way.

You are a fucking hero. Period. Let's fucking do the work so YOU can live to your highest potential!

Alright, we talked about a lot in this chapter:

- The power of gratitude!
- The power of perspective!
- The power of storytelling!
- The power of a true hero!
- The power of meditation!

Which gratitude practices have you been incorporating? Are you ready to begin your meditation practice? Set a reminder on your phone for both until you remember to practice them naturally. These small practices will help you connect with the Universe in such a powerful way, you'll be feeling some major shifts ASAP.

The rest of the list is still important. Just know that YOU are the hero and that your perspective and how you tell your story matters.

I have so much confidence in you, and I know that you're really ready to put in the effort to show your Sugar Daddy that you care.

CLEANING THE HOUSE

Alright, so we've talked about how a little extra love, appreciation and time go a long way... Now it's time to clean up the house.

Let's say you and Sugar Daddy are doing well and he wants to come over and make you dinner at your new apartment that he's paying for. The doorbell rings, and your handsome Sugar Daddy is standing there with groceries in hand, dressed in your favorite dapper attire. His hair is combed nicely and he's even got a bouquet of flowers for you. You open the door and smell his luscious cologne. You welcome him in and invite him to have a seat anywhere he would like.

He turns around the room, looking for a place to sit and his smile slowly turns into a frown, his nostrils begin to flare, his eyes start to water, and his mouth shrivels up to make the most disgusted grimace you've ever seen him make, and then with two swift steps he walks right out the door he came in.

You take a look around now too, wondering what has gotten into him, and see that there's actually nowhere to sit. Every square inch of your apartment is covered in trash; crumpled chip bags, candy wrappers, to-go boxes, empty soda cans, old moldy food, animal hair, spilled drinks, cigarette butts, all the gifts he's given you, clothes, and other hoarded items sprinkled in between. Sugar Daddy was going to try and cook you a nice dinner, but thank goodness he left after seeing the living room because the kitchen is 10 times worse! Rotten food everywhere, cat litter box overflowing (why is your cat litter even in your kitchen anyways?!), spilled spoiled milk, and the trash can has overflown into a large pile that has encompassed a whole corner. In order to find the trash you would have to climb the dump mountain first.

Sugar Daddy probably ran out of your apartment with that horrible look on his face because he didn't want to throw up due to the awful smells.

And more than that, what do you think he thinks of you when you're living like a complete slob kabob? He probably won't want to continue dating you much less continue doting on you!

You can't have a clean mind in a dirty house. You can't have clean energy in a cloudy mind. Without clean energy and a clean house, your Sugar Daddy, the Universe, won't be able to give you its many blessings.

We're all after the same things: ABUNDANCE, PEACE, HAPPINESS AND FREEDOM.

All of which come from a state of FLOW.

And if you want to be abundant, happy, peaceful and free, you'll need to be making big monayyy off of your Sugar Daddy, meaning you gotta GET IN THE FLOW.

Imagine a very peaceful river, flowing easily and gently down the side of a mountain. The water is calming and the sound of it could probably make you fall asleep.

A leaf falls from a nearby tree and gently floats down the river, following every bend until washing up on the riverbank in a colorful pile of fallen leaves.

The water flows with ease and the leaf has a gentle trip.

Imagine the river is a flow of energy with the Universe and the leaves are the little miracles and blessings the Universe is delivering to you. If there were a hundred logs in the way, the leaves might never make their way down the river.

Flow can't happen in a chaotic environment.

Energy needs a place to move so that it can flow in and out with ease.

Money is just energy!! So if you want more money, you've gotta clean out the crap that's blocking your flow.

If you're ready to clean out the crap, there are several aspects of cleaning to consider:

1. Clean your environment; house, bedroom, car, wallet, purse, and all the physical spaces around you. If you're unfamiliar with how or why having a tidy space is important, I highly recommend Marie Kondo's book, *The Life-Changing Magic of Tidying Up.* She's helped millions of people change their lives by cleaning up their space. Even if you don't do it all in one go, just start by cleaning up a little tiny bit. Just tidy up your wallet, your bedroom and one other space you spend time in most. When things are clean you'll have clearer thoughts and it will be easier to get into the flow state that is absolutely necessary for money, energy and happiness to flow in.

2. Clean your energy; once you've cleared out the physical shiz, you can use sage to smudge, or clean, the energy of your room, house, car, or anywhere you think the energy needs some cleaning. You can use sage or palo santo, or you can just visualize bright white light cleaning the energy in the room and allowing the negative or stagnant energy to be released.

3. Clean your body; shower, eat healthy foods, breathe, exercise. It's soooo important to exercise because it

is one of the best ways to release the stagnant energy that builds up in the body. Yoga and breathwork are also very useful for releasing old energy and emotions in the body.

4. Clean your mind; avoid watching negative things such as the news. Meditate, journal, and clear the mindspace to create more room for abundance to flow in. This includes doing your shadow work, and releasing the old negative emotions and trauma from the past! We will talk more in depth about shadow work later.

When our space is clean and our minds are clear, the Universe's messages will be easier to hear. When you clean your space, your energy, and your vibration, you open yourself up to receive all the blessings the Universe has been trying to gift you.

ARE YOU LISTENING

Most people probably believe the Universe isn't talking to them, but the truth is that THEY are just not listening! A great byproduct of cleaning your mind is that your listening skills will be enhanced. When you tune in, it's just like turning the dial on a radio and getting to the right station. If your radio is turned to the wrong station and all you hear is static, you don't just listen to the static, you play around with the knob to tune into the right station. Clearing your energy and the energy around you is just like tuning your radio to the right station, which helps you get into flow more easily.

If your radio is off, you'll need to turn it on first. How, you ask? By actually taking ACTION. Don't just read this book and say it was good. I want you to actually implement these tools I'm giving you so that you can turn your radio on and get it tuned into the right channel.

The Universe IS here for you. If you refuse to open your mind and listen up, you only have yourself to blame for where you are today.

It's time to turn that radio on and tune in to the Universe's channel for you. Take responsibility for your life and for your actions and get started now!

Start by deciding when you are going to clean. Put it into your calendar. Then decide when you're going to meditate and set yourself a reminder. Even if you only meditate for one minute, it still counts.

The word PROSPERITY comes from the word prosper which apparently comes from the meaning: to move forward with hope.

So as long as we keep MOVING FORWARD WITH HOPE we are prosperous.

The only time we are poor is when we run out of hope.

Before writing this book, I went through a rough time and accumulated a lot of debt. I was working at a club to get by and save up, but then the Coronavirus pandemic swept my entire savings away. I was hitting a newfound rock fucking bottom, and I felt so lost and alone that I almost gave up hope.

During my hopeless hour, I came soooooooooo close to seeking out a Sugar Daddy to take care of me. And to be honest, this wasn't the first time in my life that I'd prayed for some rich guy to come into my life and pay my bills and my debt. I actually have a lot of friends who are currently on the Sugar Daddy train right now, and I have no judgement for anyone who chooses that route. In fact, I used to have an older gentleman taking care of me a few years ago. He didn't necessarily pay bills for me, but whenever I needed help, he was there. Then one day I realized that the Universe wanted me to go out and create abundance for myself. I heard a voice in the back of my head saying that if I were to stay in that comfortable relationship, I would never grow into the millionaire that I was meant to become.

If I'd been still dating him when the pandemic hit, I might have been saved, but I know the Universe brought me here to share my story. The Universe has made me poor so that I can desire riches. The Universe gave me riches so I can crave my soul's purpose. And the Universe brought me to rock fucking bottom so that I could rise from the ashes. My purpose is to heal my money wounds and create an abundant life for myself so that I can share my story with you. If I were still with my Sugar Daddy, I would not have any of the words to write this book.

This book right here has saved me, and I hope it is saving you too.

Besides, we don't want to rely on a real Sugar Daddy anyways, because then we're not fully free. And let's be honest, freedom is what we're really all searching for, not just the money. We want money so we can live with ease (=FREEDOM). We want money so we can pay other people to help us with the tasks that take up our time so that we can spend more time with family (=FREEDOM). We want money so we can buy fancy gifts for our parents and host the big holiday gatherings in our mansions (=FREEDOM). We want money so we can travel the world (=FREEDOM).

I think you get the point. We want money for the freedom that it gives us. We don't just want money for the money itself.

Once again, MONEY IS JUST ENERGY. It's the freedom that we really desire.

We don't need a real live Sugar Daddy because the Universe is throwing torpedos of blessings and miracles our way, but sometimes we are just too busy with our radio unplugged to notice.

Plug in your fucking radio, dude. If you've read this far, then you're totally going to do it. I have faith in you. You don't have to change your whole entire life up. Just add in a few tiny simple changes that will grow over time.

I started with my gratitude journal back in the day, and here I am now. You don't have to switch everything up, just take a few of my suggestions and actually implement them.

An idea without action is just an idea

You got this babe. I'm one million percent betting on you. Don't give up. You will know the next right step at exactly the right time. I promise. When you decide to listen, you will be led.

FORGIVENESS

Once upon a time while I was dating that older gentleman, I decided to get day-drunk with some friends. When he came to pick me up, he was just in time to watch me down the last jagerbomb of the afternoon. I said bye to my friends, and he escorted me to his shiny silver Jaguar F type SVR convertible. He held the car door open for me, and I got inside.

On the ride to his place, he kept asking me if I was okay, which I thought was weird because I kept telling him I was. I guess I didn't realize how intoxicated I was because suddenly I was vomiting the entire contents of my stomach, including the salmon I'd just eaten, out of the car window. I was lucky the windows were open so he barely noticed. Or so I thought.

In the morning, I woke up with doggos licking my face. I was dazed and confused, and my head fucking hurt! I jumped up, realizing that I had been sleeping on the floor all night.

"Do you know what you did last night?" He asked me when he saw I'd woken up. I stood there just looking hungover as fuck with my mouth wide open. I had no idea what he was talking about.

"Well after I picked you up, you threw up all over me and my car. You tried to be sneaky and shoot it out of the window but it started flying back inside, all over me and my beautiful red seats. I sent you inside to shower and I had to spray my car down with the hose, and by the time I got in the house you were asleep on the floor. I called my detail guy who agreed that it was an emergency and made an appearance earlier this morning. Apparently there was even salmon in the exhaust pipe!"

I was mortified! I couldn't believe that I'd behaved this way. Obviously there was nothing I could do except apologize a thousand times.

And he forgave me.

It was simple.

He wasn't that mad at all. He made jokes about it for a while but he was never mad. The fact that he was able to forgive me so easily probably saved the beginning of our relationship.

In relationships, when one partner does something wrong, the other partner needs to learn to forgive them.

I'm not saying forgive everything, like when someone continues to cheat on you over and over. I'm talking about little things; like throwing up in your Sugar Daddy's nice ass car.

Life is going to happen. And there are certain things that we cannot change. We just have to learn to accept that and keep moving forward.

After my Sugar Daddy forgave me, there was one more thing that needed to be done.

I needed to forgive myself.

We all make mistakes and shit happens. Beating ourselves up over the things of the past that we cannot change is self-inflicted torture. We cannot grow from a place of low self worth. Throwing up in someone's fancy car is also not a good enough reason for me to punish myself forever.

If, in every moment, we are evolving into the best version of ourselves, we must understand that the things we have done in the past were the best that we knew to do at that time.

We only have so much space in our hearts and if they're filled with pity and self hate, we will never be able to manifest love and abundance in this life.

We have to keep the heart space open by forgiving ourselves and forgiving others. With an open heart, we have more space for energy to flow freely, hence bringing in more abundance, happiness and freedom to ourselves.

When you forgive, you free yourself.

It doesn't matter what fucked up things a person has done to you, by forgiving them you're freeing YOURSELF. It doesn't mean that the other people are not wrong, it just means that you're not going to hold onto that pain anymore.

When we release all the pain and suffering that's been weighing us down, we create more space to be free and allow love and abundance into our hearts.

This is where 'the work' really is.

It may seem like a dark world we live in, but we are beings of light.

It is so much more than what meets the eye. Although bad things are happening, good things are too. Every person who has a wound can heal, and every person who has healed can help others to do the same.

The people who have hurt others also feel pain and regret. Some of them may never learn to forgive themselves for the things they've done in this lifetime.

The thing is that everyone is doing the best that they know how to do. It doesn't mean that it's okay to hurt others, but not everyone understands how to live with love and integrity.

Imagine an innocent child who's experienced abuse all their life. Imagine if they never experienced love or kindness. This child probably wouldn't understand how to love another person, and they would probably grow up hurting the people in their lives because of their trauma. It's not their fault, but it doesn't justify their actions either. It's up to that individual to see the cycle and that it's their turn to break it.

They can grow. They can heal. They can learn. Just like you and just like me.

There are a lot of opinions about what really happens after death, but I truly believe that after this life we're born again. Some believe that our souls have multiple mates that we bounce from one life to the next with. In some lives we are happy together and in others we are the abusers or victims of one another. They say we keep reincarnating time and time again to learn all the lessons we have come to learn, and to fill our karmic debts.

This concept helps me to see that the Universe has a plan for us all.

I know that there are people in the world doing horrible things, but it is our job in this lifetime to forgive those people and save the victims with love. Moving with love is the only way to heal our world, and forgiveness is the only thing that can open our hearts.

No matter how much inner work you do, forgiveness will be one of the most important things to continually practice. It isn't always easy, but it doesn't have to be hard.

I recently learned Ho'oponopono, an ancient Hawaiian practice of forgiveness. Although I have a Hawaiian background, I hadn't heard of this concept until I learned it from Manifestation Babe Kathrin Zenkina.

There are various methods, but when I practice of Ho'oponopono, I forgive by focusing on the situation or person that needs to be forgiven and saying these things:

1. I forgive you (release the pain you're holding)
2. I'm sorry, please forgive me (I'm sorry for holding on to this pain)
3. Thank you (Thank you for the lessons that this has taught me)
4. I love you (Send love to the person/situation)

It is important to make sure that you send love in the end because that's how you *really* know you have forgiven.

Another way to practice forgiveness is by closing your eyes and imagining an energetic cord that attaches you to the person or situation that you need to forgive. This cord may be black or dark, but then take a few moments to meditate with it, imagining a giant bright white pair of scissors coming down to cut the cord. As the cord is cut, imagine that it disintegrates into golden particles of light. Imagine that these particles are love dust, sending love and healing vibrations to both parties.

If someone is still hurting you and you want to forgive them it is the same process. I find it harder to forgive someone who is currently causing me pain, but it's a practice that we can continue to learn and grow from more and more over time. Just know that forgiving someone doesn't mean allowing them to continue hurting you. Create solid boundaries for yourself and then love them from afar. Remember, forgiveness is about freeing YOURSELF. Not them.

The more we practice forgiveness, the more our hearts will open, and the more abundance we can attract. I know it doesn't sound like forgiveness will have a direct affect on your bank account but IT DOES.

If you want the Universe to take better care of you, you will have to do the inner work.

Here are some ways you can start practicing forgiveness now:

- Write a list of situations or people you need to forgive. Start with one item on your list and practice Ho'oponopono, cord cutting, or any other forgiveness ritual with it. See if you can release it from your heart so you can have more space to invite love and abundance inside. Repeat this process with as many items on your list as you can. Remember, it will take time, but it will be worth it.

- FORGIVE YOURSELF for anything and everything! Remember that YOU are the most important asset in your life or business. Without YOU, your dreams cannot come true. Start with all the little things and then forgive yourself for the big things too. We will have regrets in life. Just make the promise to yourself to learn from any mistakes or missteps, and forgive 'past you' so you can move forward and grow.

- Practice forgiving in the moment. Was someone rude to you at the grocery store? Did someone flip you off on the highway? Cut karmic cords and forgive them immediately. Life is so much more joyous when the energy is flowing freely and not getting stopped up in our heartspace.

ASK AND YOU SHALL RECEIVE

Let's imagine another scenario with Sugar Daddy. You ask him sweetly one day, "Hey, can I pretty please borrow your credit card?" And he hands it over without question.

The Universe is my Sugar Daddy because when I ask, I receive. It's called manifestation, and in order to manifest, we must learn about the Law of Attraction. It's a universal law, just like gravity, that everything in this time-space reality is based on energy and vibration. The Law of Attraction states that **like attracts like**. Applying this law to manifestation means that what we think, believe and feel determines our vibrational frequency, which determines what we attract. It's like our brain is a giant magnet for everything we think.

One Friday night a few months ago, while I was getting ready to go work at a nightclub, I was having a conversation with my friend Jose. He was just hanging out while I was 'beating my face to the gods', and he was telling me about his life and how he had been going through a tough time. He had just gotten out of an abusive relationship and he was saying that, though he's been torturing himself, he was ready to have some fun.

"Ryin," Jose said to me that night, "I just wanna have fun! I've been dealing with this bullshit for so long! I'm over it! Fun Jose is coming back! You know how long it's been since I've had a threesome?! [My ex] and I used to have threesomes but then ever since shit got crazy, all we would ever do was fight… It's been fucking foreverrrr since I've had fun like that!!"

"Yeah Jose," I agreed, "I do think that you need to get out there and let loose a little."

We laughed and then he continued to go on about exactly what he would do if he could have another threesome.

When I couldn't take the details anymore, in an attempt to end the conversation I said, "Listen man, if you want it just ask the Universe!"

"Okay," he said, throwing his hands up in the air "Universe, I want a threesome!"

And then we laughed and went on to change the conversation to something more comfortable for both of us.

The next night, Jose and I went out with some of our friends at a club down the street from my house and had an amazing time. When the club lights turned on at the end of the night, I was hungry, so some of us went to get food while the others kept partying.

The next morning, I woke up to several missed calls from Jose. *Fuck! I hope he's alright*!

I jumped out of bed to return his call, praying that he wasn't dead in a ditch somewhere. The phone rang 3 times before he finally picked up, shouting into the phone, "Ryin HOLY fUCkInG ShIT1!!!"

"Dude Jose what's up?" I yelled back, "Are you okay??"

"Yeah I'm okay! Why what happened?" Before I could respond he cut me off with excitement, "DUDE, I FUCKING HAD A THREESOME LAST NIGHT!!"

I didn't know what to say. Still groggy from waking up, I had no idea why he was so excited to tell me about this threesome of his.

"Ryin," he explained, "do you remember two nights ago when I was over at your house while you were getting ready for work? And then you told me to ask the Universe and look! Dude fucking a day and a half later! I can't believe it!'

My mouth was wide open in shock. I let out a huge laugh.

How could I forget that I had suggested asking the Universe? Of course it played out this way!

This is a real story. When you ask the Universe for something, it does everything in its power to conspire and bring it to you.

In this scenario, Jose didn't understand that he was *manifesting* a night full of fun, but that's exactly what he did. The funny part is that he manifested it with barely any effort.

I bet you've unintentionally manifested hundreds of things into your life before, but imagine if you could do it on purpose. How would it feel to understand the laws of the Universe so fully that you could co-create your own life?

What would you ask for? If you had the power to create your dream life, instead of just being forced from one stressful scenario to the next, what would you create?

What would that be worth to you?

What you focus your energy on, you attract.

When you focus on abundance, you attract abundance into your life. When you focus on lack, you attract lack.

That's it.

Manifestation is very simple but often feels difficult if we don't fully understand it.

All we have to do is ask and it is given, but we have been so conditioned in this lifetime to think that life has to be hard or that we cannot possibly deserve good things. We believe that they can't happen, or that it just couldn't possibly happen to people like us. The list of objections goes on and on, but if you've taken care of "cleaning out the shizzz" from the earlier chapter, you won't have as many negative beliefs blocking your way.

By eliminating these negative beliefs, you have the power to create your own dream life *deliberately*, starting with releasing some (or all) of the beliefs that hold us back, like the belief this life has to be hard. It doesn't!

"No pain no gain" mentality does not serve you!

I want you to understand that YOU are the only thing standing in the way of YOUR MANIFESTED DREAM LIFE.

You CAN erase any old limiting beliefs and expand far outside of your comfort zone into incredible growth and abundance.

You are the co-creator. When you put the order in, the Universe will deliver your desire right to you.

It will take some practice to retrain your mind and wipe out all of the old limiting beliefs that you are currently holding, but in reality...

There are no real blocks, only the blocks that we believe we have.

If we believe that we can ask for something and receive it, without any limitations at all, we will have already manifested that thing into our lives.

If you believe that what you see around you as your reality and that there's no way to change it, then it's going to be reaaaaaallllllllly difficult to manifest your dream life. You might get bits and pieces on accident, but there's more fun in deliberately creating it all.

The only way to control the future is to create it

So why not make it something big and beautiful and fucking awesome?! You can do this. I've done it myself, and I'm not any more special than the next person. The Universe does not discriminate. If you understand the universal laws and use them in your favor then life will turn into a wonderful game that you will enjoy playing!

The only thing that holds your desire away from you is *your own resistance*.

Ask, and then get the fuck out of the way!

With practice and time, it gets really easy. I used to practice by manifesting amazing parking spots. I would imagine a nice spot close to the door in a nice shady area. At first it took a bit of practice, but now I have an amazing parking space 99% of the time. The thing is, I don't care that much about where I park. So the *resistance* I hold there is not very strong. On the other hand, when I used to play the lottery, I would want to win soooooooooooooo badly that I would hold LOTS of resistance to it.

Resistance is how I describe having such a deep burning desire for something, that I accidentally push it away.

When we focus on money, money grows. But if I focus on *how much I want* money, what grows? My *desire*, not the money itself!

When we are so attached to the outcome of having something, it actually vibrates at the frequency of *wanting* it rather than *having* it.

When we *want*, we are focused on the *lack*. When we *have*, we won't *want* it anymore because we already *have* it.

It feels counterintuitive but we need to understand that, because **like attracts like**, we have to feel like we have it already in order to manifest it into our lives.

Ask, and then get the fuck out of the way!

This is the hardest step to manifestation for most people. Remember that manifestation is a *practice* and the goal is GROWTH, not perfection. Personally, I do it really well with certain things, and not so well with others, but I have found ways to make letting go of resistance easier.

The easiest way I've found to get out of the way is by using this little phrase that I learned from Richard Dotts. He writes short stories about the Law of Attraction and manifestation. In one of his books, *It Is Done*, I learned about surrendering and letting go of the attachment to the outcome so that I can get the fuck out of my own way and manifest amazing things.

Everything we desire is already done in the nonphysical realm. Everything we want is already on its way to us!

So ask, and then say IT IS DONE, and truly feel and believe it to be so! When you say IT IS DONE, release your desire and fully trust that the Universe is delivering it to you in the here and now.

One last and final step to keep in mind is that the Universe is conspiring to deliver your dream life to you. If you're not listening to the guidance and directions the Universe is giving you to get in place to receive it then you are going to miss out.

If you want to be a millionaire within the next 5 years, you've gotta create the strategy and let the Universe fill in the details. Your part in the action is important because the Universe will deliver you blessings and miracles through opportunities, people and events. If I ask for $100, and then my bff Liz calls me to ask if I'll help her clean out her closet for $100 and I say no, then I just deflected the blessing that the Universe was bringing to me.

It has always been my desire to become an author. I didn't have any intentions of writing a book any time soon, but I woke up one morning with this book title in my head, and I knew that the Universe wanted me to write THIS book NOW.

But if I didn't get up and put my fingers to the page, this book would not exist.

Every time I sat down, the Universe guided me through the process. Writing this book was not difficult. I just had to take the action steps necessary to make it happen.

An idea without action is just an idea.

It doesn't have to be a long and hard thing to do, just take little steps, so that the Universe can deliver to you what you asked for. As I was writing this book, the Universe was delivering these words to me, and now the Universe is delivering them to you. YOU still have to read this book in order to get the message, and I still had to sit down and write it.

Okay, back to the resistance part:

Another fun trick that I learned from *The Teachings of Abraham Hicks*, is a way to tell if I'm holding resistance to something or not.

"If I had to wait two years to have it, how would that feel?"

I ask myself this question constantly when I'm manifesting, because I know that if I can't stand waiting two years for something, then I am actually not in vibrational alignment with what I desire at all. If the answer is, "no I cannot wait," then I know that I am still vibrationally aligned with the energy of *wanting* more than the energy of *having* which equates to holding resistance! If the answer is, "yeah sure I wouldn't mind waiting," then I know that it is already on its way to me and that I am a vibrational match.

If you're holding onto the idea of something too hard, it will not manifest, so just let that shit go and move on with your life so that it can come to you without resistance.

Also, try to remember that manifestation is supposed to be fun! **By choosing to feel good in every single moment of your life, you are attracting more goodness onto yourself.** The more fun you have, the faster it works. THIS IS THE BIGGEST SECRET OF THEM ALL. The more fun you choose to have, the more fun your life will be. This life is all about having fun, so try not to complicate it too much.

Okay the simple steps to manifestation:

1. Ask
2. Release any and all negative beliefs or blocks
3. Trust that your desire is on its way to you (IT IS DONE), release resistance and align with the vibration of your desire
4. Take action!

PUBLICITY

If you are dating a gentleman much older than you, people are going to stare. They will see you together and question the relationship. When you're out at dinner, people will wonder, "Is that her dad or her DADDY?"

I once dated a man who was 33 years older than I was and I bet you could imagine the looks that I got at Valentine's Day dinner or when we were out with his friends. I was 23 at the time but he told everyone I was 26, as if 3 years really mattered. The point is that it is uncomfortable to have judging eyes on you and the opinions of others all up in your business, but honestly:

Everyone else's opinion can get FUCKED!!!!!!!

One night recently when I was about to go to bed, a girlfriend of mine texted me out of the blue to inform me that she saw one of my nudes floating around on the internet. She said that she figured I should know about it and sent me a screenshot.

My first reaction was shock, because leaked nudes is every girl's worst nightmare!!! But then I took a little bit of time to process what was really going on. I looked sexy in the photo, and the caption, "Tavares High Sluts anyone?" or something like that, honestly made me laugh. If someone wants to slut shame me by talking about my high school, PLEASE GO AHEAD! My high school reputation is THE LAST THING I give a flying fuck about. That part of my life is a distant fading memory. Whoever had the audacity to post that photo is probably still in pain from some of their own high school trauma.

Then I couldn't help but think about how much that person might be hurting on the inside to where they would find joy or comfort in tearing someone else down. I wonder if they were bullied or got their heart broken in high school and still haven't healed from it after all these years. I wonder what other traumas they must have experienced in order to pull an internet troll move like that.

Then I thought about it even more, and realized that, though I have had trauma, my life really hasn't been so bad. I love myself. I know how amazing my life is and how much amazingness is ahead of me. I know that things are always working out for me because the Universe is my Sugar Daddy and it doesn't matter what anyone else thinks. Then the words and judgements that were meant to hurt me barely stang at all.

Why should I care about the opinion of someone that doesn't even love themselves?

The stress began to melt away and a fire started burning within me. I saved the screenshot my friend sent me and posted it. HAH! Take that trolls! I used the post to speak about my experience. These people need love. They're crying out, and their soul is in pain. I know that their pain cannot hurt me, because I choose to not allow it to hurt me. Their pain is their own pain, and mine is my own. What they say about me has actually nothing to do with me at all, and everything to do with them.

What they say has nothing to do with me at all, and everything to do with them.

Read that sentence again. Understanding how to view the world from a perspective of healing and love is a major power move. I hope that everyone learns to see things this way because our perspective, like we talked about earlier, really is all that matters.

When you're dating a Sugar Daddy, people are gonna look at you. They'll gape with their mouths wide open and call you a slut, whore, or whatever, and then you'll grab the keys to the Jag and drive off, leaving those fucking haters in the dust.

Your life has everything to do with you, and absolutely nothing to do with them.

The people who are currently in your life and are important to you need to be supportive of you. They should want you to be happy and they should want to see you thriving. I have high standards for myself, personally, and I keep people in my life who respect the boundaries I have set for myself.

The only people who are offended by your boundaries are the people who benefit from you not having any.

I like to surround myself with good people. People who care about each other and the environment. I know that a lot of my friends say that good people are hard to come by, but in all reality, as soon as you stop allowing the bad birds in your life to consume you, the amazing people start coming out of nowhere.

I switched up my whole life a few years ago. I went from drinking every day to doing yoga most days of the week. I started going to acroyoga jams and became obsessed. I made friends with some vegans and started spending time with people who cared about my growth. All of this happened when I switched my environment up and stopped feeding the bad birds in my life.

Everything we feel is a reflection of our internal state, and everything *they* feel is a reflection of their internal state.

Other people who are here to judge actually don't care about your happiness. Some people will act like they care, but if they truly cared, they would just trust that you have your own life under control or offer advice without judgement.

If your Sugar Daddy pays your bills, then who the fuck is anyone else to tell you a damn thing?! Are they paying your bills? Are they going on fancy vacations? Are they living a lavish lifestyle? **Or do they wish they could, so they sit back and judge you instead, because there is a void within them that isn't being fully expressed**?

Let's get real deep for a moment: those people do not understand how to be honest with themselves, so that's why they can't express their realest, deepest thoughts with you. Instead of being vulnerable with you and talking about what's missing in their lives, their feelings come out as judgement because they don't know any other way to express what's really going on within them.

What they say has nothing to do with me at all, and everything to do with them.

When embarking on your spiritual journey, there will be people judging you. Take a deep breath with me, exhale and roll those shoulders back and down. These baby souls just need time. They might say, "you're acting different" or "you've changed."

Let's say you are trying to be more positive. Maybe one of the things you must do to protect your positive energy is stop engaging in negative conversations. When your friends start complaining or judging others, you may need to excuse yourself or try to guide the conversation to more positive topics. They might not have anything positive to say, especially if they aren't learning to stop being negative themselves. This is when the conflict within them begins to rise. They won't understand what is going on yet, and they might think that you're being weird or trying to act like you're better than everyone else.

When you choose to grow, it triggers others around you because they are then being faced with a decision: to grow with you, or to let you outgrow them. And no one wants to be left behind. This is all happening at a subconscious level, so they won't even know what it is about your new changes that's bothering them. They don't understand the ways of the Universe yet. They don't know how to listen for the answers like you're learning to do.

Some people might feel this conflict and unintentionally try to drag you down, while others will notice your positive changes and want to come with you. The latter will wonder what you're doing differently and they won't judge you because they are ready to experience their own expansion. It's a really beautiful thing to watch another person growing alongside you on your journey. It's playful to understand that we are all one and that as they grow, you grow. There is no comparison, just love.

If your friend starts growing "faster" than you and you become jealous, take a step back and notice what that feeling is about. Remember that everything we feel is a reflection of our own internal state, and jealousy often means that there's something within us that is being neglected. This judgment thing goes both ways! Don't be the friend who is unintentionally dragging someone down because you didn't take the time to go within and observe what meaning these feelings have for you. These feelings of jealousy can actually teach us quite a lot about ourselves.

My friend, Caylia, is a badass yoga teacher. She's been teaching yoga for a few years longer than I have, and she is a freaking beast! When I used to see her at acroyoga jams, she would be smiling bright and full of life. She had spectacular body awareness and could do incredible tricks that were waaayyyy out of my skill range. She could press up into a handstand, which I've always wanted to do, and everyone loved her! I loved her too, and she was a dear friend of mine, but there was this feeling of hurt that I would bubble up inside me whenever I would see how cool she was. This wasn't the first time I'd felt this. In fact, I have felt this way towards many of my friends. I hate to admit it but I used to be a very jealous person and still continue to experience these feelings often, except now I know a better way to navigate them.

So when Caylia was around, I would notice those sensations within me and then go home later and ask myself (and the Universe) what was going on. It was from this place of peace that I heard my answers loud and clear: I wanted to be like that.

The void I was neglecting at the time was my yoga practice. I didn't practice every day or meditate every day, so my energy was like ehhhh. It wasn't bad, but it was not radiant like hers.

What I realized is that I didn't really want to be more like Caylia, but more like myself. The most fulfilled, badass version of myself! So I used that jealousy as fuel to get my ass into gear and start taking action towards my yoga goals. I started meditating more and practicing yoga more often. Now when I see her, I feel 100% content with myself and happy to be in her presence. I'm proud of her, I'm happy for her, and I am proud of and happy for myself too.

Once that void within me was filled, I no longer had any negative feelings around Caylia. And it's because of my growing connection with the Universe that I understand how to navigate through jealousy now.

Your haters probably don't understand, especially if they're not becoming enlightened themselves. It's up to you to lead by example and learn to navigate your thoughts and feelings from that place of peace within.

Everything you need is already within you, and as long as you learn how to listen, you will find exactly what you need.

I can't stress enough how important it is to connect with the Universe, because with a strong connection, no one else can hurt you. From the perspective of love, the opinions of others just look like reflections of their own drama and problems bouncing off of you right back onto them.

Like I've said before, this is all just a matter of practice, and a matter of choosing to open our minds.

This is a slow and steady process. There may not always be a huge shift that we can physically feel. It's not like one day you wake up and you're like, "Holy fucking shit I'm enlightened now, I feel different!"

What really happens is you learn something new and grow from it, and then learn something else and grow from it. Maybe you teach someone how to heal, share a bit of love, and then after you take a look back, you'll say, "WOW, what a difference!"

When I was in high school, I smoked weed every day. When I was in high school, I did not meditate or talk to the Universe or practice yoga regularly. When I was in high school, I spent most of my time getting high, smoking cigarettes and partying with my friends. My connection to the Universe was basically non-existent. I used to post pictures of me doing a headstand and hashtag "yoga" and I even got a tattoo of the OM symbol, but I didn't put anything spiritual into practice.

Back then I thought that one day, I'd stumble upon a monk who would take me under their wing and show me the way. They'd say "I've seen a light within you, Child, and you must save the world." And then I'd follow everything they said and blossom into a beautiful healer.

I tried to just live my regular non-spiritual life, with hopes of one day being led by a spiritual teacher who saw a light within me. What I didn't understand was that the teacher was actually within me all along, and that through reading, writing, meditating, making the right investments in mentors and coaches, and (mostly) connecting to the Universe, I would learn to lead myself.

I have now blossomed into a beautiful healer, not because of one major shift that changed my life, but because of the daily commitment to my journey, and the daily commitment to my connection to the Universe.

What's far more important than how anyone else is going to see you is how you see yourself. Understand that you CAN practice expanding your power! It's all inside of you, just start by releasing it little by little until you fully bloom!

I never had rich parents and I hated it. I hated them for not being able to buy me the things I desired, but now I see that they've given me an even greater gift that I was neglecting to see all along. My parents gave me unconditional love and the promise to never stop loving me no matter what I ended up doing with my life. When I went to jail they said, "Do you think that because of this, that we love you any less?" I am now understanding that this love has actually helped me more than money ever could have.

It's taken me years to get to this point, and now I see that the biggest blessing I could have ever received was the fact that my parents didn't care if I got a college degree or not. They don't care if I make a million dollars or ten dollars. They don't care if I travel the world or stay in the same house for the rest of my life. They don't care if I date a 55 year old man or work as a stripper, because my parents still love me the same. I can write a crazy book called, *The Universe is my Sugar Daddy*, and know that I am still loved and accepted in my parents' eyes.

The way my parents love me is the way the Universe loves you.

The Universe doesn't see all of your insecurities.

The Universe doesn't see all of your fuck ups.

The Universe is here to love you unconditionally and have your back 100% of the time. And not to mention the fact that the Universe is infinitely abundant too.

Not having rich parents inspired me to want to get rich on my own. Not having rich parents helped me along my path so much more than I could understand back then, but as I grow, so does my new understanding of how everything in my life has happened FOR me, not TO me.

I've manifested abundance. I've manifested this amazing rich juicy life. I have everything I could ever want because I chose to connect with the Universe. I asked, took action, and then received. It's that simple. I didn't let the opinions of others get in my way. I just took a stand, and I never sat down. I mean, some things in life have knocked me down, but I promised myself to never stay down for too long, and I always stood back up.

I invite you to do the same. Make the commitment. Start practicing gratitude every single day. Practice meditation at least a couple times a week. Clean your energy and your space, learn more, love more and never stop growing. This is the only way to not care about what other people have to say or think about us. The more we connect, the less relevant their opinions will be. The people who are meant to stay in our lives will understand how important our happiness is and they will be here to help us grow.

"Be who you are and say what you feel, because those who mind don't matter and those who matter don't mind"

-Dr Seuss

TRUST

What's the difference between 99% and 100%? The answer is not 1%, in fact, the answer is actually: a 100% difference.

If you're a monogamous lover, and you're in a committed relationship, do you want to be cheated on? I think the answer is no! You want a partner that is 100% committed to you, not 99%. If they're nice to you and do everything you want in a relationship 99% of the time, but the other 1% they're off cheating and lying behind your back, you would not be pleased.

Now imagine you're dating your Sugar Daddy who is committed to you 100%, but for some reason you just don't trust him. He is honest, faithful, trustworthy and he has never done anything to make you doubt his loyalty. How do you think that he would feel if you accused him of taking other sugar babies out on dates to spoil them?

Sugar Daddy would be HELLA offended, maybe even hurt, that you don't trust him! Especially after all that he has done for you. I'm sure he doesn't want to be accused of things that he would absolutely never do!

In order for that relationship to work, you have to trust him, especially if you want to keep getting an allowance!

If you want to manifest unlimited divine wealth from the Universe, your Sugar Daddy, you are going to have to trust!

Luckily for us, the Universe IS the most trustworthy Sugar Daddy anyone could ever ask for. There will be no lying, no cheating, and no stealing. Just 100% love and commitment all the time.

No matter what you ask for, the Universe will either respond with one of two answers:

1) Yes

OR

2) Wait, I have something better.

When something isn't working out, just trust that it is. Don't freak out, because that low vibrational 'freak-out energy' will deter whatever is on its way to you. Sit back, relax, and trust that the Universe always has something amazing up its sleeve. Understand that THINGS ARE ALWAYS WORKING OUT for you, *whether they feel like they are or not.*

One cool way to practice trust is through daily affirmations. I have this one written down on sticky notes posted all over my bedroom, car, notebooks, journals, and house:

THINGS ARE ALWAYS WORKING OUT FOR ME

Write this down 25 times a day. Say it aloud or in your head over and over again. Do whatever you have to do in order to help you reprogram your mind to trusting in the Universe 100,000%.

Things are working out for you. They always have and they always will, so allow it to flow.

Whether things are good or great, it's still working out for you. The difference is your energetic addition to the equation.

What are you focusing on? What are you allowing in?

If you're still focusing on what went wrong, then your energetic addition to the equation is taking away from how amazing it could turn out in the end. So instead of being FUCKING AMAZING maybe things will turn out just okay.

If you're focusing on the things that went right, then things might turn out even more amazingly for you!

When things are "just okay" it's time to practice looking at the bright side!

I was having lunch with my mom the other day and she was telling me a story about how her boyfriend had been rear-ended recently. She said how he was bummed out at first, but then a lawyer helped him to win $1200 from the accident so he was able to go pick up this other car from a town a few hours away. He had been trying to save up to go get the car and now he has enough! At first it looked like a shitty situation, but the Universe had a plan! And the end result was better than he could have expected it to be!

A similar situation happened to me a few years ago when I rear-ended an older Russian couple in the car in front of me. Luckily for them, their car had barely even a scratch; but my car was totally FUCKED! The whole front bumper was smashed. I have no idea how their car was totally fine. They yelled at me in Russian for a minute and then we pulled over into a nearby parking lot. We called the cops and, as we waited, I was starting to build up with anxiety.

"FUCK. I literally cannot afford this right now!"

I knew from previous accidents that rear-ending someone equates to a $150 ticket, and then on top of that it would be a $500 deductible to fix my car.

While we were waiting for the cops to show up, my friend called me and told me that she was about to go to work at a strip club. She said I could come with her and probably make enough money to fix my car and pay the ticket.

I had never danced before. I had no idea what to even think. All I knew was that my boyfriend at the time would definitely not condone something like that.

I prayed for an answer and I told her that I would get back to her. The hours went by... 2 hours, then 3 more hours... We waited for 5 whole hours for the cops, but it turned out that they were too busy to come report our accident.

So, the Russians and I came to an agreement. I gave them my insurance information and went home. On the bright side, I got out of going to work that day and I didn't get a $150 ticket! My car was still screwed, but I just had this deep feeling of trust that it was all going to work itself out.

The next morning, my boyfriend came to pick me up so we could go to the springs. I stepped outside my apartment building and I noticed one of my neighbors inspecting my car.

"This your car?" He asked me.

"Yes..." I answered hesitantly.

"Yes yes my name Vito and I fix for you." He said in his deep foreign accent. "Bring to my shop and call insurance. I waive your deductible if you bring to me instead of whoever you bring to."

I was shocked! Not only did I not get a ticket, but I also didn't have to pay to get my car fixed!

Everything worked out better than expected, all because I didn't freak out. I trusted that the Universe had a plan for me, and I followed the right next steps.

The Universe is always cooking up some magic for you, 24 hours a day, 7 days a week. The Universe does not take a break from blessing you. What we have to understand is that each blessing comes in a different shape or form, and some are often disguised as something else. When shit looks like it's hitting the fan, don't freak out! That just means that there are more blessings coming your way!

Don't stand in the way of your success by stooping down to a lower frequency like worry or stress. Because that equals you standing in the way of your abundance. YOU deserve this amazing beautiful life so please get out of your own way and allow in your freedom. You got this. I have faith in you.

One more story: During the COVID-19 pandemic, I lost my job at a nightclub where I was making loads of money. It's funny because I told the Universe that I was done with this industry of work and then, well, it happened much sooner than I had expected. I had enough money saved up to last a while, and at first I thought that we would be locked down for about two weeks. NOPE! I'm still in the midst of the pandemic while writing this right now, lol.

As my savings were holding me afloat, I told myself that I would be able to go back to work as soon as everything cleared up.

SURPRISE: My club burned down! In the middle of a pandemic!

Not only did my job get shut down due to COVID, but my place of employment no longer even existed.

"What am I going to do?"

At first I panicked and had a quick cry sesh, but then I heard the message from the Universe loud and clear.

The message was that I needed to stop treating my coaching business like a "side business" and start acting like the Boss Goddess CEO that I am.

Through the times of financial struggle, I always found my way to center and peace in the end. I trusted in the Universe to never let me down, and it never has.

Throughout the last couple of months, I've had a deep fear of running out of money, deeper than I've ever experienced before. All of my credit cards were maxed out completely, I had to borrow money from friends, and I was really really struggling. I ate rice and beans for two weeks straight, just trusting that I would somehow make enough to pay my bills.

Things always worked out. Right when I was at the very last straw, I saw the light at the end of the tunnel. I started making sales in my business and I was able to pay everyone back.

Life was great and getting greater, and the Universe took care of me again and again and again.

Sometimes life feels like a test of whether I can keep on trusting when things feel rocky, and now I know that I will always pass those tests. My faith is so strong and I encourage you to find the same strength when you don't know what the outcome will be.

I have always been taken care of and it's not because I have good luck. I'm sharing this with you because I believe in you, and I know how powerful you truly are. You will create massive changes in your life with the concepts in this book. Commit to them 100%. Why not, right? Show the Universe how serious you are about the new life you're creating. Show the Universe how much you love having him as your Sugar Daddy, and see how much allowance you get...

HONEYMOONING

You and Sugar Daddy really hit it off, but after a few months the butterflies start to go away. Maybe he stops buying you things or maybe you stop paying him attention. Everything you were doing in the beginning of the relationship to please one another has been put on the back burner.

This happens in a lot of relationships, and when it does, that's usually when the couple has to come together to make a very powerful decision:

Are you both going to try harder to make the relationship work or should you let these issues break you up?

When it gets to this point, a lot of questions will come up. Is the relationship even worth working on? Can you two really get back to how things once were? What are you doing differently, and where did you get complacent with one another's needs? If you really try harder, can you make this all work out together?

True love doesn't last forever, but you can create it with the same person over and over and over again.

When the honeymoon phase ends, it's up to both parties to try and rekindle the love they once had.

Don't just meditate or journal for a week and stop. You can't just read a couple of self help books, say "Okay, I'm enlightened now," and put the rest away forever!

Spirituality is a constant practice. And our connection to the Universe is only just beginning.

I was talking to someone earlier today who was telling me about a problem they were going through, and they kept asking me questions like, "What do you think about that? What does that mean? What should I do? Do you think this is a good idea for me? Do you see me like this..." But I know they already knew the answers to all of those questions. What he needed was to just TRUST himself, and trust in the Universe. I asked him if he had thought about journaling it out, and he replied with, "Man I just feel like I'm so over that.. Like I've done that sooo much already..."

Listen, I'm telling you, there's never a time when you'll be done working on yourself. It's like if I put gas in my car, run it to E, and then get upset because I already put gas in it. Like duh there WAS gas but I used it all! The same goes for inner work. You're always gonna need to refill that tank and you'll always have more inner work to do!

It doesn't matter what you did last week, and it doesn't matter what you did last year. If you haven't meditated or journaled today then all your past meditations and journaling won't help you with your problems NOW!

If you forget to meditate for a week, the Universe will still be here for you. You can always come back and rekindle the love, but don't expect abundance 24/7 if you're only going to take care of your spirit just every once in a while. If you want to get you an allowance from the Universe allllllllll the time, you need to fully commit!

There is always inner work that can be done, and we can always learn to connect to the Universe more deeply. I've even experienced many shifts within myself, even throughout my time writing this book, and I can't wait to come back and read it in 10 years just to observe how much I've grown. I choose to be someone who's continually learning and growing, and I invite you to find ways to do the same.

Remember that life is about the journey, not the destination.

Do you know anyone who only comes around when it's convenient for them? The type of person who is always there when you're giving out help but then they're nowhere to be found if you ever needed them? Right, those kinds of people are not the best kinds of friends! In this amazing Sugar Daddy relationship, you don't want to be this type of person. Just keep the relationship going forever! Be there for the Universe because the Universe is ALWAYS there for you!

If you read this book and didn't make any changes in your life, maybe you weren't ready. I trust that you'll come back again in a few months or years when you ARE ready to embark on this journey. Know that the Universe is always here and will continually bless you until you return. It's up to you to open yourself up to receive.

You don't have to change up your whole life and you don't have to stop doing the things you love. I don't want anyone to think that because they're not ready to "get their shit together" the Universe is just going to have to wait. You can take tiny steps now and you can do the work at your own pace.

But if you don't start small now, time will pass and *you will wish* you started listening to the Universe sooner. You could end up wishing you started your daily meditation practice "back then," or you could start NOW and be grateful you did.

Like me, I spent many years coming up with excuses of why I couldn't meditate until I finally chose to *just start*. And now I'm so grateful I did.

It's up to you. Life is a series of choices and the choice is always yours. How you choose to see each situation and how you choose to react will create the story and how you choose to tell it is alllllllll up to you.

This is your story now and you get to write it however you want!!!!!!!

JUST BE YOURSELF

I've spent a lot of my past drunk, high, and a lot of other things people might judge me for, and I'm still a damn fucking good ass person and a kick ass healer, coach and spiritual leader!! Don't think that you need to fit into some type of "spiritual persona" or change who you are in order to make the Universe your Sugar Daddy. You don't need to be anything more than you are RIGHT NOW.

It is important to observe your behaviors because what you DO will reflect what you THINK, and what you THINK is what you will continue to CREATE for yourself. If you're not loving what the Universe is currently delivering, aka you're broke and you're ready for some damn allowance already, you will probably have to change some things. But that doesn't mean that you need to be any *more* than you are right now.

The Universe sees you as pure and complete, a bright being of light, because that is what you are and the Universe is going to love you unconditionally no matter what.

What you choose to do while you're here on this Earth is up to you, and if you want to start seeing amazing manifestations of abundance in your life, and allowance from Sugar Daddy then YOU need to discover and clear your blocks to let the light in.

Just because you don't necessarily make "good choices" all the time does not make you less worthy of the Universe's love. You will always be loved.

For example, if you smoke a lot of weed AND you know that you need to start meditating, you can make the commitment to yourself that you will add a meditation practice to your day and choose to wait until after you meditate before sparking one up. This way incorporates your new commitment to the Universe, while not forcing you to make changes that you don't want to make. This small step may be all you need for the stage of growth you desire right now, and it's just that, a step.

If you believe that weed is the devil's lettuce and that your life is better without it, then quit smoking and dive into this spiritual game head first! It is up to YOU to follow your own internal guidance system and listen to the cues the Universe provides. If you can't hear the cues, it's time to start changing up some behaviors that will help you LISTEN to the guidance that is already there.

Furthermore, I don't want you to think that becoming "spiritual" means you're not allowed to party or have fun anymore. In fact, I love to party! What I'm saying is that it is of more value to my whole life and future to be *intentional* about everything. For instance, when I partake in mind altering substances, I ask the Universe to bless them to the nourishment of my body, mind, and soul. I ask for guidance and protection, and I never take more than a recommended dosage. THERE IS NO REASON TO GET FUCKED UP JUST TO BE FUCKED UP.

I used to drink for the sole purpose of getting drunk, while now I JUST drink with my friends when I'm out for fun. I'm 25 years young and I don't want to give up late drunken nights yet. Until I am, I know that the Universe supports me and loves me no matter what I do, and I know that I am making daily commitments to honor my authentic self, my limits and the Universe at all times. There is absolutely no reason to go *past* our limits, so find your limit and honor it!

Drugs and alcohol are just *magnifiers* of what you have going on within you. If you're deeply unhappy, the substances may make you feel good for *a brief moment*, but since that inner work STILL needs to be done, eventually your shadows WILL come out!

I made a new friend recently who told me a story about how she had a really bad LSD trip and went into a dark hole that she couldn't escape. She ended up getting baker acted and woke up in the psych ward. I shook my head at first and said, "Girlllll, I'm sorry that happened to you, but you must have taken waaaayyyyy too much."

Before I could finish she cut me off to tell me the rest of her story. A few weeks later while she was in Cali trimming weed, she took a THC edible and got waaaayyy too high. On this marijuana high she found herself in that same black hole from the LSD again. Only this time when she came back to her senses she was in the hospital with 7 very large open gashes in her leg. From this dark shadowy place, she somehow stabbed herself in the leg with trimming shears and was rushed to the hospital.

She doesn't remember doing this at all. All she remembers was waking up in the hospital and that dark place that she never wanted to see again. That day, she vowed to take her mental health VERY seriously. When I met her, she said she only wanted to focus on good vibes and making her mental health a priority, and after hearing this story I completely understood why.

If you have darkness within you that is yearning for light, *you need to take care of that* before EVER trying to use alcohol or anything else to cover it up!!! This is an extreme story and it's important that you understand this because, unlike a lot of other spiritual teachers, I do not push sobriety onto my students. I believe that certain people can responsibly partake while others cannot, and that is all dependent on each individual's personal goals, needs and desires. Not to mention, I make it a very strong point in my teaching to help my students follow their own intuition instead of expecting me to just tell them what to do. Trust yourself. Doing what other people say to do without following your internal guidance system first is laziness and spiritual bypassing.

When someone pretends they're doing the work but they're not, that's spiritual bypassing. These people, instead of doing the actual inner work and becoming one with the light, use their horoscope, oracle cards, and other spiritual guidance as an excuse for acting the way they do. We can't just say, "Oh well I'm a Gemini so I can't change who I am," or blame the Mercury retrograde or the psychic reading we had last month for our problems with no intentions of actually solving them. EVERY PROBLEM CAN BE SOLVED.

IT IS OUR RESPONSIBILITY TO DO THE INNER WORK. Bottling up our emotions just creates a bigger problem down the line. And using mind altering substances as a bandaid for the problems we are bottling up is the WORST thing we can do!

When you pop the cork off of a champagne bottle after you shake it, what happens? An explosion of bubbly, right? That's basically what you are doing to yourself emotionally when you bottle up what's going on inside you and then adding drugs or alcohol to the mix is like shaking the bottle.

Eeek! Wouldn't you rather just open the bottle without shaking it first?

The interesting thing about working on the dark shadowy parts of ourselves is that it's never really as scary as we think it is going to be. A lot of healers call this "shadow work" and I love that term because in the end that's really all those dark parts are: shadows.

Imagine that you're running away from something. It's night, you're scared, and that thing chasing after you backs you up into a corner. You're frightened and you're dripping with sweat, you have goosebumps! You're sooooo terrified, but after a moment in that corner without feeling anything stabbing or biting you, you finally turn around and open your eyes. As you shine your flashlight on the dark figure, you see that it was your own shadow all along.

Shadow work is just shining light onto the shadows so they simply disappear.

This journey to the light doesn't have to be scary. In fact, some shadow work is really fun! Just commit to uncovering whatever shadows come up for you along your journey. You will know that there is work that needs to be done when you feel negative emotions. For example, in the story I told earlier about Caylia, I realized I was feeling jealous, which meant that I needed to uncover what piece within me needed more light.

Some people have experienced a lot of trauma, and like we talked about in the 'Cleaning the House' chapter, the majority of shadow work will likely focus on shining light on those traumas. If there are things you are having trouble clearing, you can seek out help. Look for a local (or online distance) reiki healer, hypnotherapist, NLP practitioner, healer, reader, psychic, life coach, therapist or so on.

It's okay to seek help, just make sure that you have tried doing the work yourself FIRST and that YOU are strengthening YOUR OWN INTUITION *before* seeking help.

When I was 3 years old, my parents moved our little family from Burbank California to a very quaint small town in central Florida called Mount Dora. We lived in a house down the street from some distant relatives and, as I grew, I noticed that our family was not like other families because of what was going on behind the scenes. These differences impacted my life tremendously but I can now see that it all had a very strong divine purpose.

My parents had been regularly visiting our distant relatives as their "spiritual advisors". They saw them every week for many years of my life. I understand now that my parents only did what they thought was right, but throughout these years, they allowed the advisors to manipulate and control every decision they made, including the way they decided to parent us as kids.

My brother, sister and I didn't really think much of it at first, just because we were so young, but then after some years we started to notice the weird things, like how my parents got rid of most of their possessions because "the things held bad energy" and out of nowhere decided to become very strict in the way they were parenting us. They changed their names to their "spirit names", which caused chaos for the rest of our extended family, whom we weren't allowed to see anymore. These changes, among many other details, were very painful for me at the time.

When I was in elementary, middle school and high school, I was the sweetest kid. I was in honor classes and my sole obsession was band class. I never skipped a day of school because I knew that if I skipped school, I would miss out on band. Yes, I was a band nerd!

Then one day, after an amazing summer of band camp between my sophomore and junior years, my parents informed me that I was no longer allowed to participate in extracurricular activities. "Get your head out of the clouds," they said and forced me to get a job.

This particular event was the most devastating for me, considering how important my band community and my future in all-things-band-related were to me. My entire plan for college was based around getting a music scholarship of some sort.

This event was the first major shift in the trajectory of my entire life and the worst part was that I knew that my parents didn't make this decision themselves. They were just the puppets and we can all guess who was really running the show behind the scenes.

That year I lost all my friends. I had spent all the past school years of my life only associating with band people, but they didn't understand why I had to leave so they called me "quitter" and it hurt me too much to sit with them at lunch knowing that I wouldn't get to spend any time practicing with them in class.

I was lonely and sad, and at 16 years old I chose to turn to weed. I started smoking with the girl across the street and decided that I was going to fit in where I could: with the potheads. I spent the rest of high school getting high every day before school and skipping class to get high.

As soon as I turned 18, I moved out of my parent's house. Now I can see that I was searching for freedom all along, the freedom that I didn't have at home, especially when my controlling parents were being controlled themselves. I see now that smoking weed was not only a coping mechanism, but also a way to escape.

My parents chose to listen to guidance outside of their own. My parents didn't take responsibility for the life they were living and creating so they allowed outside influences to dictate their every move.

Now that we're all past that phase of life and everyone in my family has escaped, healed, or learned to cope with what we now call the "cult", we've each individually grown stronger from it. The biggest lesson I've learned is to ALWAYS trust my intuition.

YOU ARE ALWAYS RESPONSIBLE FOR YOUR LIFE. YOU MUST ALWAYS BE AT CAUSE FOR EVERYTHING. NO MATTER WHAT ANY HEALER OR SHAMAN TELLS YOU TO DO, YOU WILL HAVE THE CHOICE TO FOLLOW THEM OR NOT.

As a spiritual teacher and guide myself, it is a HIGH PRIORITY for me to teach my students to follow their own internal guidance system! Always *always ALWAYS* trust your higher self and the Universe before trusting someone else!

If it doesn't feel right, get the fuck out of there!!!!!

When you're seeking spiritual help, ALWAYS follow your intuition FIRST. Don't make the mistake that my parents made. They started opening their mind and followed the first spiritual guides they encountered. I'd like to say my parents may have been gullible or maybe they were just in too deep before they realized how bad things were getting. Maybe they were too lazy or too scared to trust themselves and hence chose to give all of their power away.

Honestly, I stuck my head in the sand for a long time when it came to what happened with my family. I used to bottle up those feelings and emotions and push them waaayyy back down. I've been learning to work through these shadows and take responsibility for my part.

Remember that it is up to us to tell the story. If it weren't for my crazy past, I would not have been able to write this book. If it weren't for the "cult", I would not have had this trauma to heal from or be able to help others heal from theirs. I may have become a teacher or spiritual guide who told my students *what to do* instead of asking *what they feel* had I not been forced to trust my intuition so strongly as a kid. If it weren't for that trauma, I may have fallen into the same trap my parents did while they were on their search for "more". Now I get to use what could have become a weakness as one of my strongest strengths while guiding others along their own righteous paths on their journey to peace, love, and abundance.

I chose to escape through band and school, and when band was taken away from me, I found other ways to escape. I spent a lot of my young adulthood partying and bottling up my traumas, emotions, and feelings of unfulfillment with where I was in my life. I used substances to feel connected to the people around me and discovered that everyone is escaping from something just like I was. The most important lesson we can learn is to face our fears head on. No one is perfect, but we are still exactly enough, and exactly where we are both supposed to be right now. We really don't need anyone or anything to make us feel whole or to tell us what we need to do. We are already whole right now.

When turning to spiritual help, I have always been skeptical because of my own personal trauma. I didn't even fully believe in the power of hypnosis until AFTER I hypnotized my first 3 clients! Even though I am usually apprehensive at first, I still always seek out help when I need it. Having another perspective or another person's energy to help me clear my shiz is very effective and much faster than clearing it all on my own.

I have plenty of inner work to do, but I don't let it stop me from sharing my beautiful and perfectly imperfect light with the world.

Do your shadow work. Practice forgiveness. Love yourself how and where you are *right now*! Follow your heart, listen to your gut, and remember you fucking got this!!!

THE UNIVERSE IS MY SUGAR DADDY

I wrote this juicy book to help you enhance your connection with the Universe because I spent so many years of my life wishing that a Sugar Daddy would come save me, and help me escape from all the SHIT that I was doing to myself.

I finally made the choice to be responsible for my own vibration and my part in the creation process and now you have the opportunity to make this choice for yourself, too. Regardless of all of my flaws, insecurities, bad decisions, and good decisions, I still get to choose to be a good person and deeply connect to the Universe every single day. This is a choice that I have committed to, and I pass this high vibe baton on to you.

I now get to receive all the abundance, opportunities, allowance, freedom and joy that I've been waiting for this whole time and I could never have written this book without the help of our Sugar Daddy, the Universe.

LIFE IS SHORT, BE YOURSELF.

FUCK WHAT ANYONE ELSE HAS TO SAY ABOUT YOU.

THIS IS YOUR ONLY LIFE. LIVE IT FULLY.

YOU ARE EXACTLY WHERE YOU ARE SUPPOSED TO BE.

RIGHT HERE. RIGHT NOW.

THINGS ARE ALWAYS WORKING OUT FOR YOU.

AND EVERYTHING YOU DESIRE IS ALREADY ON ITS WAY.

ABOUT THE AUTHOR

Ryin Amber Lokietz is a master manifestation expert and leading spiritual mindset coach, certified NLP Practitioner, Hypnotherapist, yoga instructor, intuitive healer and light worker. She started her spiritual journey as a child when her parents were involved in a cult and she began learning to trust her own intuition at a young age. Because of this experience, she chose to develop a direct relationship with the Universe, rather than only listening to the advisement of other people and spiritual guides.

This is not one of those cookie-cutter or one-size- fits-all types of spiritual books. The Universe is my Sugar Daddy was written so that, like Ryin, each reader can learn to follow the beat of their own drum while still creating marvelous momentum for their own manifestations and spiritual journey.

For more visit www.ryinamber.com
or follow me on instagram:
@ryinamber

Printed in Great Britain
by Amazon